Preface

La Lumière de Français au Monde is a series of seven course books that has been designed for the students of middle school of India and abroad. This is intended to help the students, practice their knowledge of French vocabulary. This book offers to teachers and students an innovative and creative approach for teaching and learning the foreign language.

Some artworks has been included to make learning French easy in a play way manner. For the beginners, this book should be of value. As this book is prepared in pictorial and graphical manner. The vocabulary is used along with articles which indicate the gender of nouns. So that, students can learn whether the noun is masculine or feminine. The difference between formal and informal has also been mentioned by using different subject pronouns.

I am making learning a language fun with this book. This book will help students to learn French through captivating exercises and activities. The lessons and activities inside this book are developed by the help of language and education experts. Every page of the book is adapted for children who are not familiar with the language at all. The book is designed for parents and children to work together and learn a new language the fun way.

In this book, the knowledge about France has been presented in a geographical manner. For the better understanding of our kids every sentence, every noun has been written in English and French both. Images has selected as per the level of students. Each and every lesson has short exercise for the practise of students. Course is divided into two parts. After each part there is one big exercise for the revision of all the previous work done in previous months. That can give confidence to students.

This book helps kids understand the basics of the French language. These basics challenge their comprehension while enjoying the lesson taught. Learning French language has never been so easy... just try this simple book out.

Table of Contents

Lesson 0 (Leçon 0): Knowing France (Connaissez la France)

There are seven continents in the world. ·

1. Australia

2. Asia

3. Europe

4. Africa

5. North America

6. South Africa

7. Antartica

France is situated in Europe.

The capital of France is Paris. Another name of France is « L'hexagone » because of its shape which is in the shape of

Another name of Paris is « La ville lumière » which means the "City of light" because it was the first city in Europe to use gas lighting to illuminate its streets. At present day Paris has over 50,000 street lights.

The flag of France is tricolour flag known as « Le Drapeau Français »

The three colours are blue, white and red. France is famous for the following things:

*Monument : La Tour Eiffel

*Museum : Le Louvre

*Cheese : Le Camembert

Monuments (les monuments)

La Tour Eiffel

Le Sacré-Cœur

L'Arc de Triomphe

La Tour Montparnasse

Le Louvre

Le Mont Saint-Michel

À Vous

Exercise 1: Colour the French flag. (Coloriez le drapeau Français.)

Exercise 2: Draw the Eiffel tower. (Dessinez La Tour Eiffel.)

Lesson 1 (Leçon 1): Alphabet (L'alphabet)

A (ah)	Ananas (ah-nah-nah)	 Pineapple
B (bay)	Banane (bah-nahn)	 Banana
C (say)	Ciel (see-al)	 Sky
D (day)	Dent (dahn)	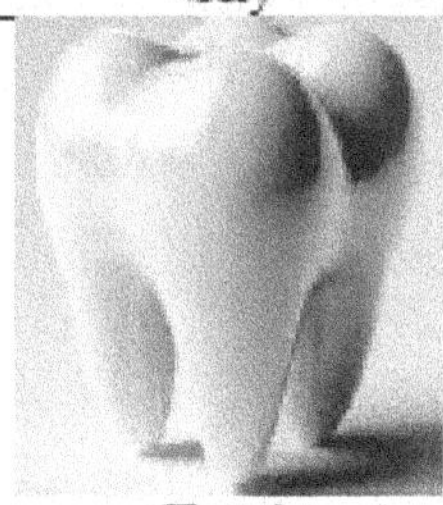 Tooth
E (euh)	Ecole (ay-kol)	 School
F (eff)	Fromage (phrho-mage)	 Cheese

G (jay)	Girafe (jay-raff)	 Giraffe
H (aash)	Hache (aash)	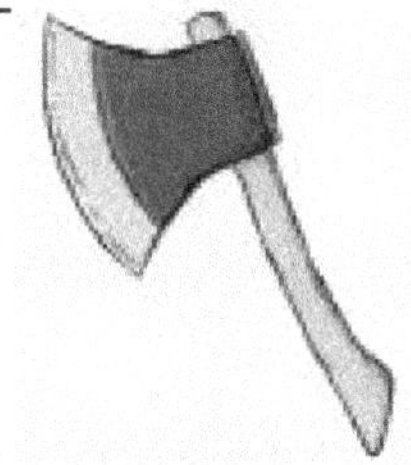 Axe
I (e)	Igloo (ee-glu)	 Igloo
J (ji)	Journal (zur-naal)	 Newspaper
K (ka)	Kiwi (kee-wee)	 Kiwi
L (ell)	Lion (lee-ohn)	 Lion

M (emm)	Mer (meh-r)	 Sea
N (enn)	Nounours (noo-noo-rs)	 Teddy bear
O (oo)	Ovale (oh-vah-l)	 Oval
P (pay)	Pigeon (pee-ghon)	 Pigeon
Q (ku)	Queue (ki-eu)	 Queue
R (air)	Raisins (rei-zen)	 Grapes
S (ess)	Soleil (so-layi)	

		Sun
T (tay)	Tigre (tee-greh)	 Tiger
U (eu)	Uniforme (eu-ni-formh)	 Uniform
V (vay)	Voiture (vwah-tyur)	 Car
W (dooble vay)	Wagon (va-gohn)	 Wagon
X (iks)	Xylophone (zee-lo-fohn)	 Xylophone
Y (igrek)	Yeux (yeo)	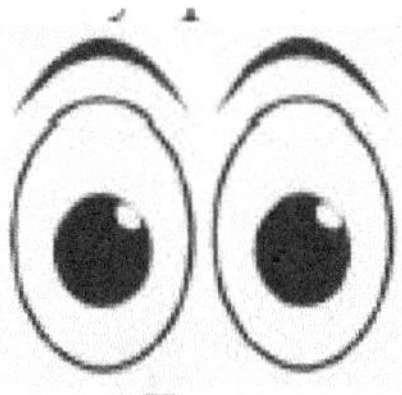 Eyes
Z (zed)	Zoo (zoo)	 Zoo

Exercise 1: Match column A and column B. (Liez le colonne A et le colonne B.)

Colonne A (English)	Colonne B (French)
Car	ananas
Sky	tigre
Pineapple	fromage
Axe	soleil
Kiwi	école
Tiger	voiture
Eyes	kiwi
Sun	ciel
Cheese	hache
School	yeux

Lesson 2 (Leçon 2): Let's count together! (Comptons ensemble!)

Numbers in French (Les nombres en français)

Number	English	French	Image
1	One	un	
2	Two	deux	
3	Three	trois	
4	Four	quatre	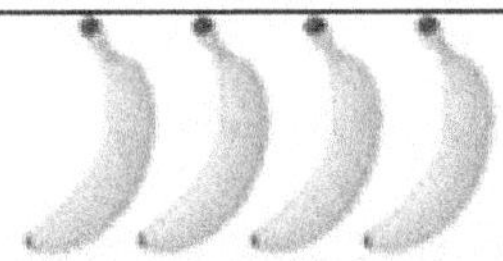
5	Five	cinq	
6	Six	six	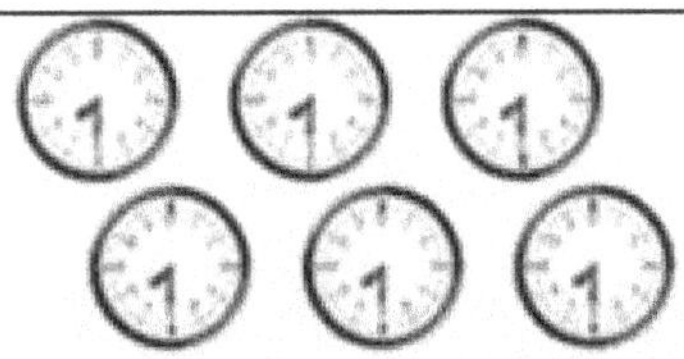
7	Seven	sept	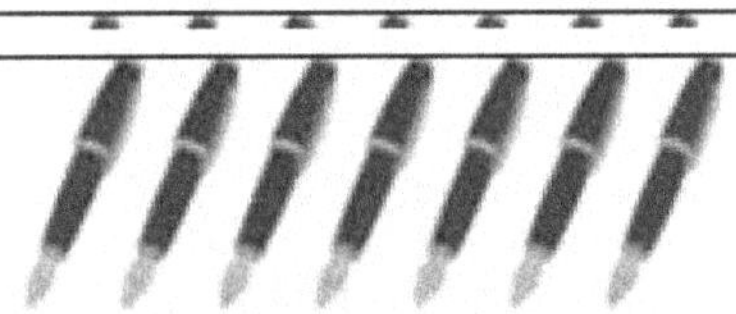
8	Eight	huit	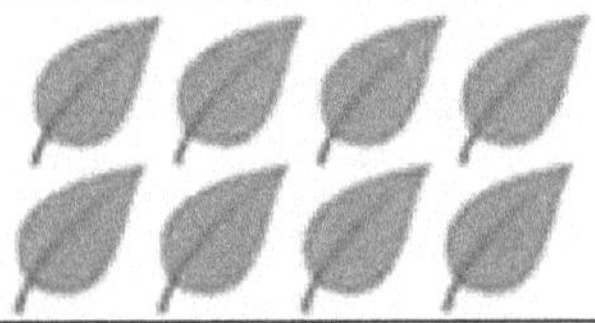
9	Nine	neuf	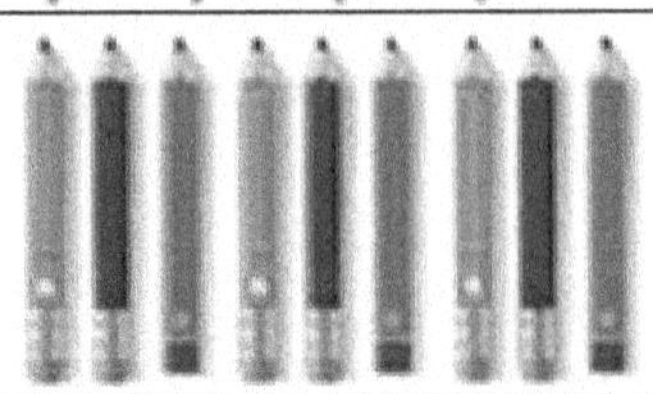

10	Ten	dix	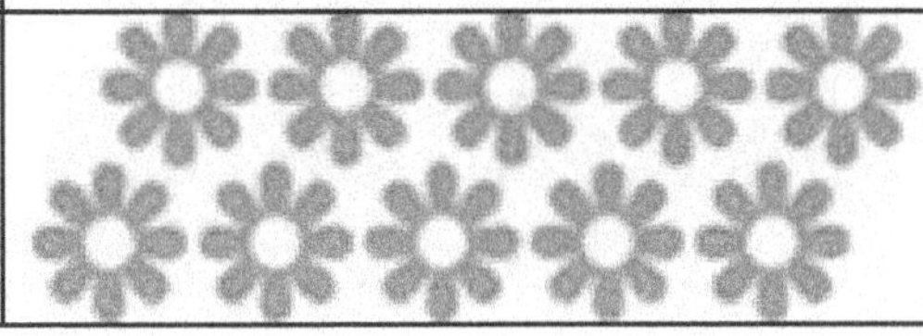

What is the time? (Quelle heure est-il ?)

Time in Number	Time in English	Time in French
1:00	It's one O'clock.	Il est une heure.
2:00	It's two O'clock.	Il est deux heures.
3:00	It's three O'clock.	Il est trois heures.
4:00	It's four O'clock.	Il est quatre heures.
5:00	It's five O'clock.	Il est cinq heures.
6:00	It's six O'clock.	Il est six heures.
7:00	It's seven O'clock.	Il est sept heures.
8:00	It's eight O'clock.	Il est huit heures.
9:00	It's nine O'clock.	Il est neuf heures.
10:00	It's ten O'clock.	Il est dix heures.

Exercise 1: Count and write. (Comptez et écrivez.)

____

____

Lesson 3 (Leçon 3): How to greet? (Comment saluer ?)

Greetings for adults (Salutations pour les adults)

Image	English	French
	Good Morning	Bonjour
	Good Afternoon	Bonjour (When leaving)
	Good Evening	Bonsoir
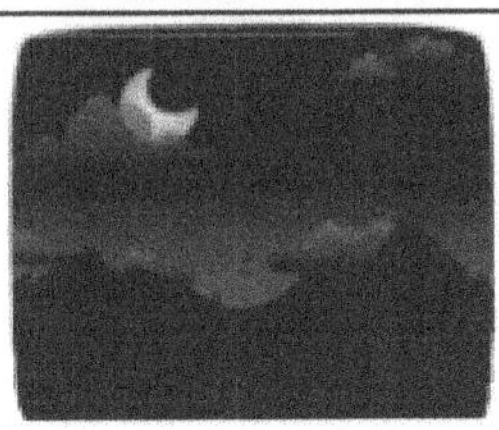	Good Night	Bonne Nuit

Greetings for friends (Salutations pour les amis)

Hi Salut/Coucou

Bye Au revoir

Note: To greet any person, student must check if the person is elder or younger.

Subject pronouns (Les pronoms sujets)

It's a pronoun which we can use in place of noun (name of a person, place or thing).

English **French**

I ⟶ Je

You → Tu

He → Il

She → Elle

We → Nous

You → Vous

They → Ill

They → Elles

Note:

You (Informal)	Tu
You (Formal)	Vous
They (Masculine)	Ils
They (Feminine)	Elles

Exercise 1: Match column A and column B. (associez le colonne A au colonne B.)

Colonne A	Colonne B
Je	You
Tu	They
Il	I
Elle	He
Nous	They
Vous	She
Elles	We
Ills	You

Lesson 4 (Leçon 4): How to introduce oneself? (Comment se présenter?)

Informal conversation (Conversation Informelle)

What is your name?	Comment tu t'appelles?
My name is.	Je m'appelle...
What is your age?	Quel âge as-tu?
I am............years old.	J'ai............ans....
Where do you live?	Où habites-tu?
I live in.....	J'habite à...

Formal conversation (Conversation formelle)

What is your name?	Comment vous appelez-vous?
My name is.	Je m'appelle................
What is your age?	Quel âge avez-vous?
I am............years old.	J'ai…………..ans..

Where do you live?	Où habitez-vous?
I live in	J'habite à..

Points to remember:

1. Start the conversation by greeting words. (Given in the previous lesson 3.)

2. The way of asking questions makes a conversation formal or informal without any change in the answers.

Now, do conversation with your friend. (Faites la conversation avec votre ami.)

Chinmay :	Hi! (Salut!)
Tanvi:	Hi! (Salut!)
Chinmay:	What is your name? (Comment tu t'appelles?)
Tanvi:	My name is__________, and you? (Je m'appelle ________, et toi?)
Chinmay:	My name is Chinmay. (Je m'appelle Chinmay.)
Tanvi:	What is your age? (Quel âge as-tu ?)
Chinmay:	I am_______years old. And you? (J'ai______ans. Et toi?)
Tanvi:	I am 10 years old. (J'ai 10 ans.)
Chinmay:	Where do you live? (Où habites-tu?)
Tanvi:	I live in Bangalore. And you? (J'habite à Bangalore. Et toi?)
Chinmay:	I live in______ (J'habite à________)
Tanvi:	Bye. (Au revoir!)
Chinmay:	Bye. (Au revoir!)

With the help of above dialogues, students can prepare their own dialogues with their friends.

You : ____

Your friend : ____

You : ____

Your friend : ____

You : ____

Your friend : ____

You : ____

Your friend : ____

You : ____

Your friend : ____

You : ____

Your friend : ____

Lesson 5 (Leçon 5): Let's go to school! (Allons à l'école!)

Today, Neha is going to school. She is packing her bag and wondering what things to put in her school bag. Here are some of the things that she can carry in her school bag.

English	French	Image
Pen	Le stylo	
Pencil	Le crayon	
Eraser	Le gomme	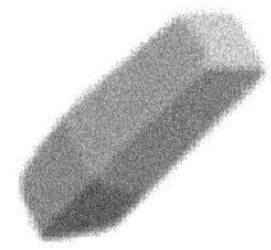
Sharpener	Le taille-crayon	
Scale	la règle	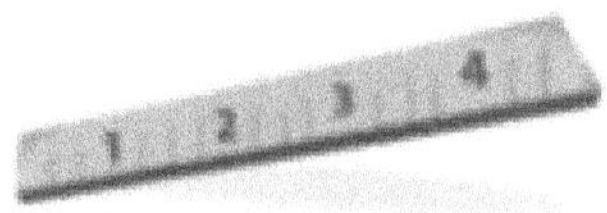
Book	le livre	

Notebook	le cahier	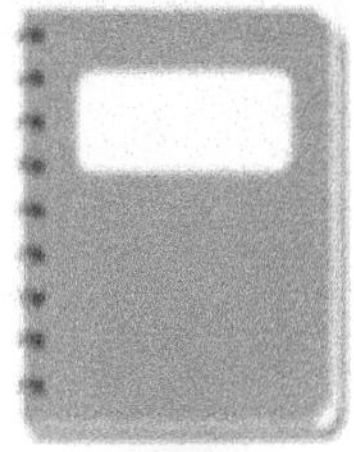
Bottle	la bouteille	
Lunch Box	la boîte de repas	

Exercise 1: Identify the objects and write their names. (Identifiez les objets et écrivez leurs noms.)

____

____

____

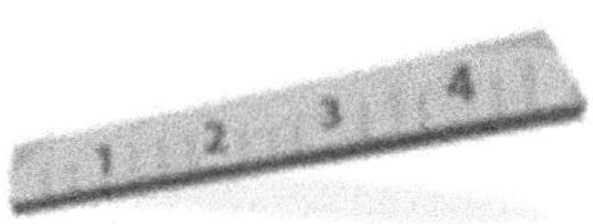

____

Lesson 6 (Leçon 6): At home (À la maison)

Today, we are at Neha's home. She is showing us her house.

Living room
Le salon

Bed room
La chambre

Kitchen
La cuisine

Bathroom
La salle de bain

Toilet
Les toilettes

Garden
Le Jardin

Objects that we can find in a house. (Des objets que nous pouvons trouver dans une maison.)

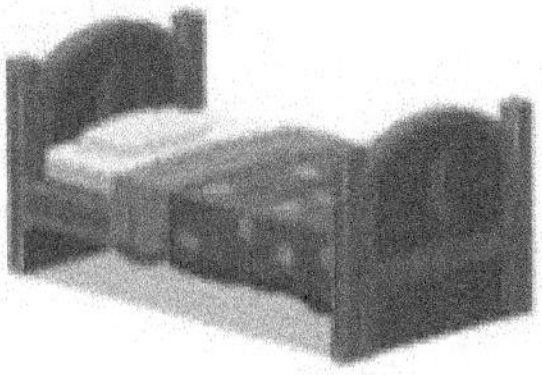

Bed
Le lit

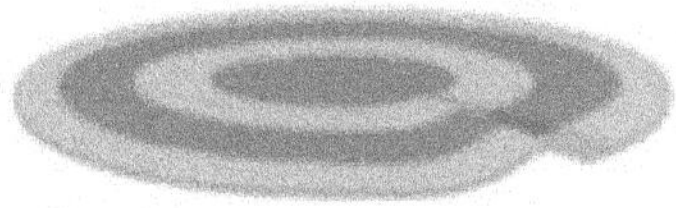

Carpet
Le tapis

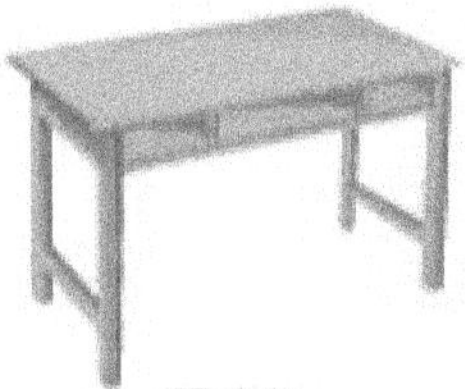

Table
La table

Chair
La chaise

Table lamp
La lampe

Sofa
Le canapé

Almirah
L'almoire

Cup board
Le placard

Exercise 1: Find the word. (Trouvez le mot.)

Correct word	Word (Mot)	Image
	TIL	
	IPSTA	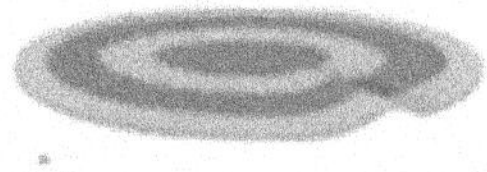
	AIJDRN	
	SCEIHA	
	MBCARHE	

Lesson 7 (Leçon 7): Food (La nourriture)

Today, Neha is going to the market to buy some fruits and vegetables. Things that she is seeing in the market are listed below.

Fruits (les fruits)

English	French	Image
Apple	La pomme	
Mango	La mangue	
Banana	La banane	
Orange	L'orange	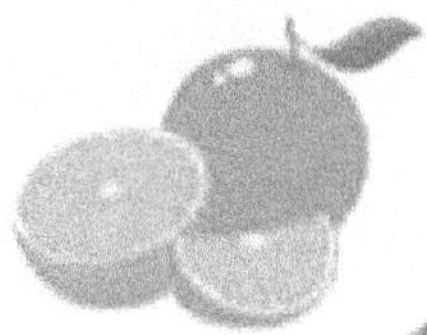
Litchi	Le litchi	

Vegetables (les legumes)

English	French	Image
Potato	La pomme de terre	
Tomato	La tomate	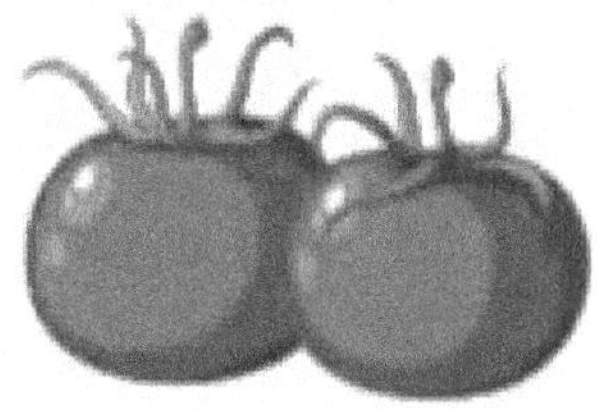
Peas	Les petits pois	
Onion	L'oignon	
Spinach	Les épinards	

Exercise 1: Find the names of fruits and vegetables from the grid. (Trouvez les noms de fruits and des légumes de la grille.)

J	L	Z	P	C	I	U
O	I	B	O	N	T	Y
A	T	O	M	A	T	E
G	C	R	M	D	X	U
K	H	A	E	M	E	G
P	I	N	L	R	V	N
O	I	G	N	O	N	A
H	F	E	Q	S	W	M

Answer: (La réponse):

A) ______________________________

B) ______________________________

C) ______________________________

D) ______________________________

E) ______________________________

Lesson 8 (Leçon 8): Animals and birds (Les animaux et les oiseaux)

Today, Neha is visiting the zoo and seeing the name of the animals written in French.

Some of them are given below.

Animals (Les animaux)

English	French	Image
Horse	Le cheval	
Cow	La vache	
Rabbit	Le lapin	
Sheep	Le mouton	
Dog	Le chien	
Cat	Le chat	
Bear	L'ours	

Birds (Les oiseaux)

English	French	Image
Crow	Le corneille	
Duck	Le canard	
Parrot	Le perroquet	
Owl	L'hibou	
Sparrow	Le moineau	
Hen	Le poulet	
Peacock	Le paon	

Exercise 1: Colour the parrot. (Coloriez le perroquet.)

Let's recall-I (Rappelons-I)

Exercise 1: Write the names of the objects in French by seeing the images. (Écrivez les noms des objets en français à l'aide des images.)

A 

B 

C 

D 

E 

F 

G 

Exercise 2: Answer these questions: (Répondez aux questions :)

A. Write another name of France. (Écrivez l'autre nom de la France.)

____

B. Write one monument of France. (Écrivez un monument de la France.)

____

C. Write another name of Paris. (Écrivez l'autre nom de Paris.)

____

Exercise 3: Read the sentences and indicate True or False. (Lisez les phrases et indiquez Vrais ou Faux.)

Sentence (La phrase)	**True (Vrai)**	**False (Faux)**
A << Ananas » means tooth.	________	________
B Another name of France is "L'hexagone".	________	________
C«Lapin » runs very fast.	________	________
D World has five continents.	________	________
E << Pomme >> means apple.	________	________

Lesson 9 (Leçon 9): The calendar (Le calandrier)

Today, Neha's teacher has given a task to all the students to count the number of days in a year. So, according to them:

There are seven days in a week. These are: Il y a sept jours dans une semaine. Ce sont :

Il y a - There is / There are

The days of the week (Les jours de la semaine)

English	**French**
Monday	Lundi
Tuesday	Mardi
Wednesday	Mercredi
Thursday	Jeudi
Friday	Vendredi
Saturday	Samedi
Sunday	Dimanche

There are twelve months in a year. These are: Il y a douze mois dans une année. Ce sont:

The months of the year (Les mois de l'année)

English	**French**
January	Janvier
February	Février
March	Mars
April	Avril
May	Mai
June	Juin
July	Juillet
August	Août

September	Septembre
October	Octobre
November	Novembre
December	Décembre

Exercise 1: Fill in the blanks. (Remplissez les vides.)

A) L_N_I

B) D_MA_CH_

C) JU_LL_T

D) _AI

E) _ÉC_MBR—

F) A_R_L

Exercise 2: Answer the questions. (Répondez aux questions.)

A. How many days are there in a week? (Il y a combien de jours dans une semaine ?)

____

B. How many months are there in a year? (Il y a combien de mois dans une année ?)

____

Lesson 10 (Leçon 10): Family (La famille)

Neha lives in a big family. There are ten mcmber in her family

Let's see bow to call them in French.

Family
(La famille)

Grand parents
(Les grands-parents)

Parents
(Les parents)

Uncle and aunty
(L'oncle et la tante)

Neha and her brother
(Neha et son frère)

Cousins
(Les cousins)

Grandfather (Le grand-père) Grandmother (La grand-mère)

Father (Le père) Mother (La mère)

Exercise 1: Paste tbe photo of your family and write your relation with your family members in the boxes by using an:ows.(CoUez la photo de votre famille el ecrivez votre relation avec les membres de votre famille dans les bol'tes en utillsant les rayons.)

Lesson 11(Leçon 11): Fcstivals of France (Les fêtes de la France)

This year Neha visited France with her family. She saw different types of celebrations there in France. Let's sec her experiences.

English	French	Image
New year	Le Nouvel An (Le 1er janvier)	
Shrove Tuesday	Le Mardi Gras	
Easter	Le Paques	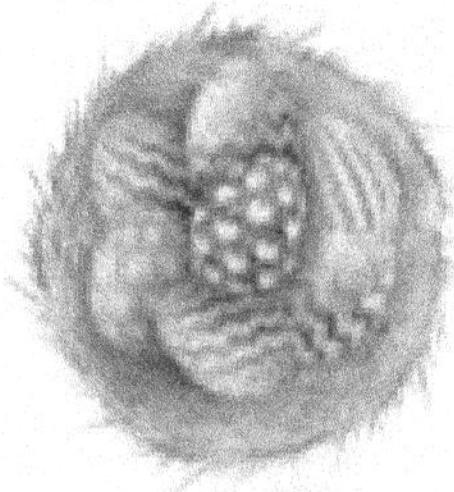
Mother's day	La fête des Mères	
Father's day	La fête des Pères	
Christmas	Le Noël	

Exercise 1: Decorate the eggs for Easter. (Décorez les œufs pour le pâques.)

Lesson 12 (Leçon 12): Colours of the world (Les couleurs du monde)

Today, Neha went to the supermarket to buy a dress for herself. There, she saw so many beautiful colours.

English	French	
	Masculine	Feminine
Blue	Bleu	Bleue
Green	Vert	Verte
Black	Noir	Noire
White	Blanc	Blanche
Violet	Violet	Violette
Orange	Orange	Orange
Yellow	Jaune	Jaune
Pink	Rose	Rose
Red	Rouge	Rouge

Note: In French the colours also have a gender. It depends upon the gender of the noun which form to use.

Example – La voiture noire.
Le stylo noir.

Exercise 1: Draw the following coloured flags and write colour's name in French. (Dessinez les drapeaux suivants coloré et écrivez le nom de la couleur en français.)

I. The Indian flag

(Le drapeau indien)

II. The French flag

(Le drapeau français)

The name of colour in French. (Le nom de la couleur en français.)

A) **B)**

C) **D)**

E) **F)**

Lesson 13 (Leçon 13): Parts of the body (Les parties du corps)

	English	French		English	French
	Head	La tête		Hair	Les cheveux
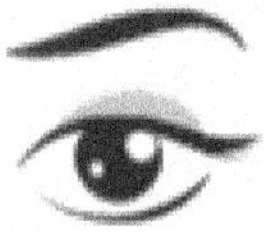	Eye	L'œil		Ear	L'oreille
	Lips	Les lèvres		Teeth	Les dents
	Hand	La main		Nose	Le nez
	Leg	La jambe		Foot	Le pied

Exercise 1: Identify the parts of the body. (Identifiez les parties du corps)

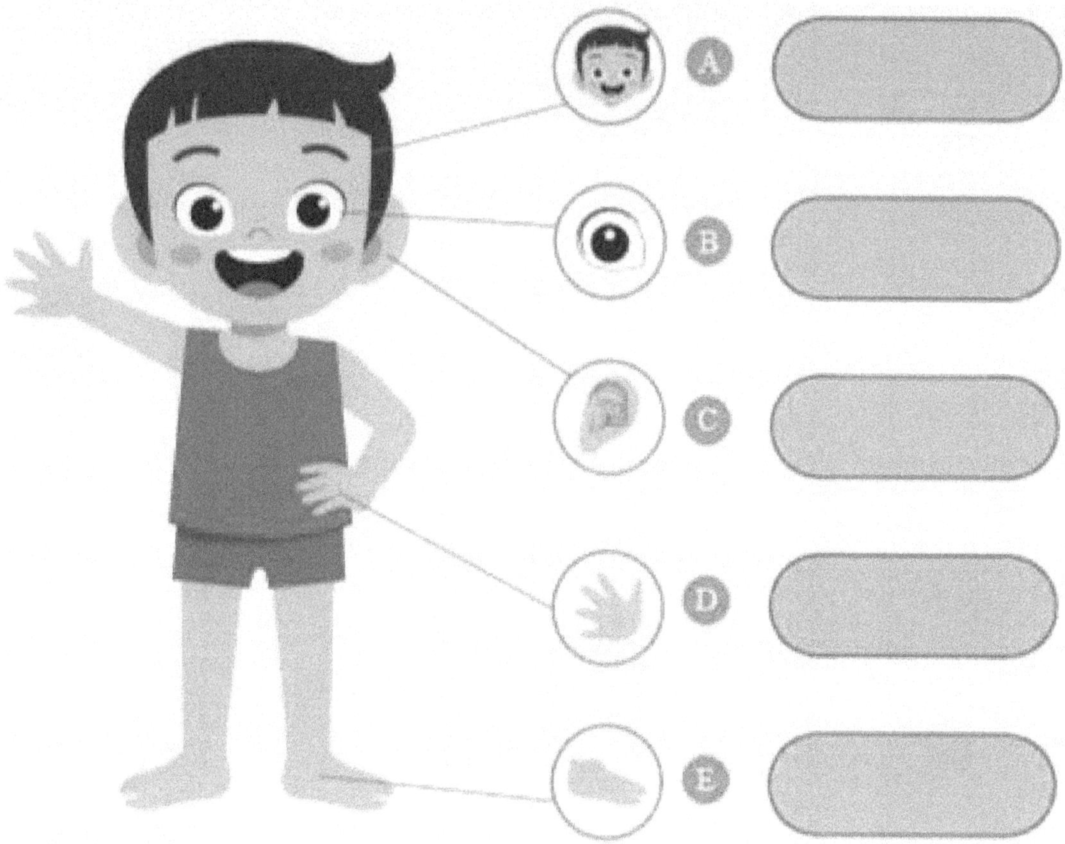

Lesson 14 (Leçon 14): Professions (Les professions)

English	French

Doctor | Le médecin

Teacher | L'ensignante

House wife | La femme au foyer

Business man | L'homme d'affaire

Plumber | Le plombier

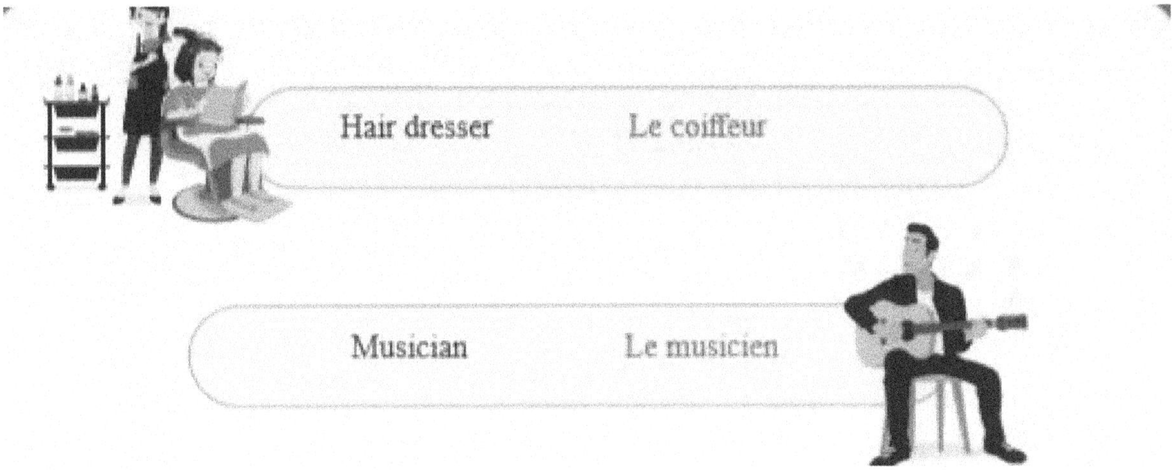

Some professions that we can see in our school.

Professions at school (Les professions à l'école)

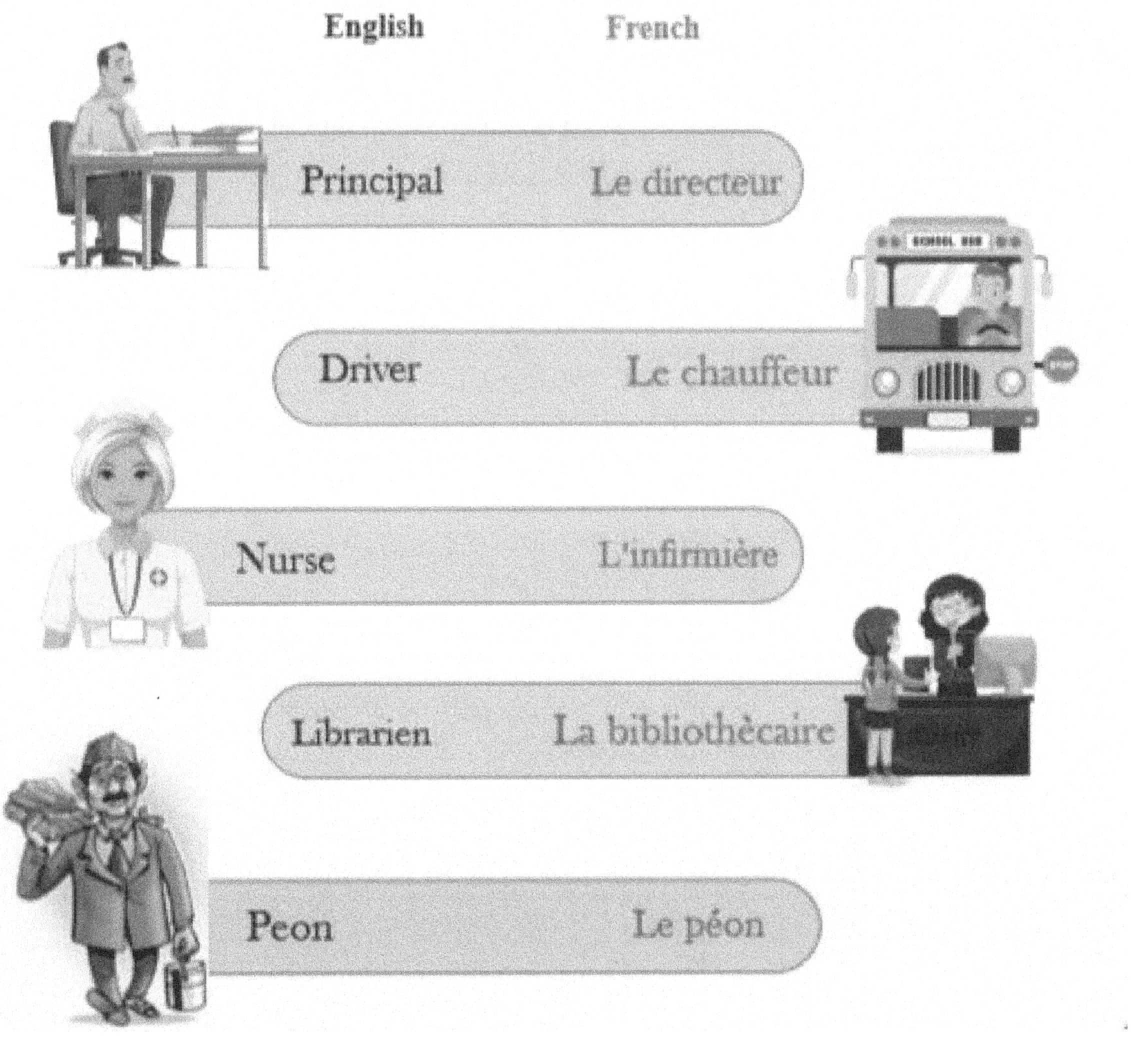

Exercise 1: Match the profession with the image. (Associez le profession avec l'image.)

Les professions

A

B

1. La femme au foyer
2. L'infirmière

C

E

3. Le médecin
4. Le chauffeur

D

F

5. La bibliothécaire
6. L'ensignante

Lesson 15 (Lecon 15): Sports (Les sports)

In the school of Neha, teacher is asking about the sports that students like Let's see how many sports are played in Neha's school.

Indoor games (Les jell' d'interieur)

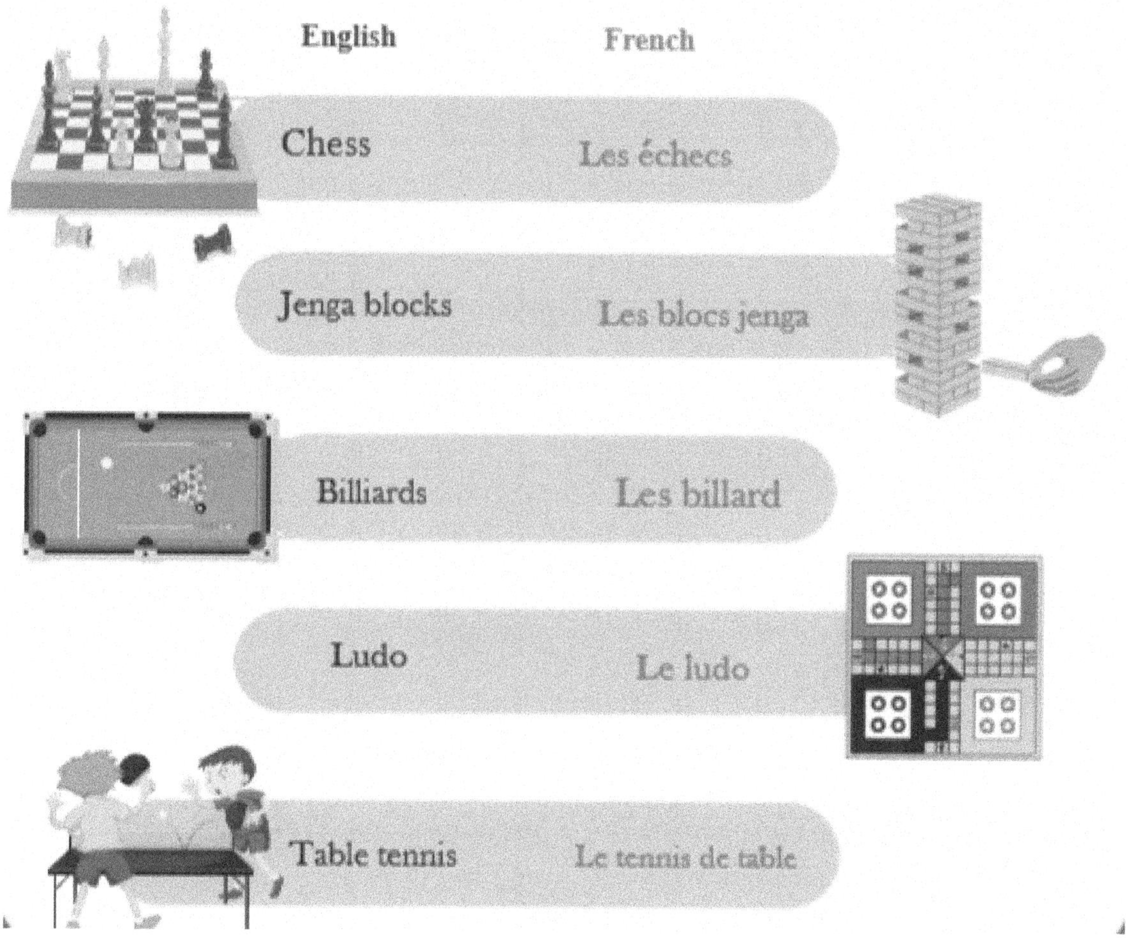

Outdoor games (Les jeux d'extérieur)

English	French	Image
Hockey	Le hockey	
Swimming	La natation	
Basket ball	Le basket ball	
Football	Le foot	
Cricket	Le cricket	

Exercise 1: Imagine that it's sports day in your school and paste the photos of the students who received prizes in the games that are played in your school.

(Imaginez que c'est le jour de sports dans votre école et colez les photos des étudients qui ont gagnés dans les jeux joues dans votre école.)

Lesson 16 (Leçon 16): Clothing (Les vêtements)

Dresses of the women (Les vêtements des femmes)

English	French
Skirt	La jupe
Long dress	La robe
Shirt	La chemise
Saree	Le sari
Heels	Les talons

Dresses of the men (Les vêtements des hommes)

English	French	Images
Jacket	La veste	
Shirt	La chemise	
Pants	Les pantalons	
Shoes	Les chaussures	

Exercise 1: Fill in the blanks with dress's name. (Remplissez les tirets avec le nom de vetement.)

Exercise 2: Fill in the blanks with dress's name. (Remplissez les tirets avec now de vetement.)

Lesson 17 (Leçon 17): Means of transport (Les moyens de transport)

Today, Neha and her friends are on a road trip. They are seeing different types of transports.

English	French
Car	La voiture
Bus	Le bus
Cycle	Le vèlo
Truck	Le camion
Train	Le train
Auto	L'auto

Exercise 1: Riddles! Solve, if you can. Write the answer in French.
(Énigmes! Résolvez, si vous le pouvez. Écrivez la réponse en français.)

A. Most of the time my papa drives. It has four wheels. It is of many colours.
(Answer: _______________)

B. We don't have to drive, we can sit, we can lie down and sleep. It's too long.
(Answer: _______________)

C. This vehicle stops frequently for many stops. You go to school by this.
(Answer: _______________)

D. It's two wheeler. You can ride it without any license, in any age.
(Answer: _______________)

Let's recall-II (Rappelons-II)

Exercise 1: Write the name of the image in the given box in French.

(Écrivez le nom d'image en boite en français.)

A  ____________

B  ____________

C 

____

D  ____________

E  ____________

F 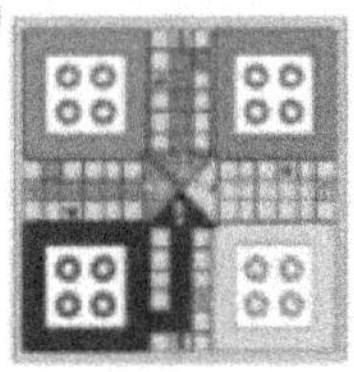 ____________

G  ____________

H  ____________

I  ____________

Exercise 2: Answer these questions: (Répondez aux questions :)

A. The day which comes after Monday. (Le jour qui arrive après lundi.)

B. The month which comes before May. (Le mois qui arrive avant mai.)

C. Name the shortest month of the year. (Nommez le plus court mois de l'année.)

Exercise 3: Read the sentences and indicate True or False. (Lisez les phrases et indiquez Vrais ou Faux.)

Sentence (Le phrase)	True (Vrai)	False (Faux)
A. **Dimanche** means July.	________	________
B. **Noël** means Christmas.	________	________
C. House wife is L'homme d'affaires.	________	________
D. Lady nurse is infirmière.	________	________
E. **Pomme** means apple.	________	________

Answers (Les réponses)

Leçon 1

Exercise 1: A-6; B-8; C-1; D-9; E-7; F-2; G-10; H-4;1-3; J-5

Leçon 2

Exercise 1: A- sept; B- trois ; C-cinq; D-huit; E- un

Leçon 3

Exercise 1: A-3; B-8/1; C-4; D-6; E-7; F-8/1; G-2/5; H-5/2

Leçon 4

Exercise 1: salut; Chinmay; 10/dix or any age; Any city's name

Leçon 5

Exercise 1: A- La gomme; B- Le crayon ; C- Le taille-crayon; D- La règle

Leçon 6

Exercise 1: A- LIT; B- TAPIS ; C-JARDIN ; D- CHAISE ; E- CHAMBRE

Leçon 7

Exercise 1: A- OIGNON; B- POMME; C- TOMATE; D-MANGUE; E- LITCHI

Leçon 8

Exercise 1: Colour the parrot in a attractive manner. (Answer may vary.)

Rappelons

Exercise 1: A-Le moineau ; B- La pomme de terre ; C- La table; D- Le stylo; E- uniforme; F-Le cahier; G- Le Banane; H-Le chat; I- Bonne nuit
Exercise 2: A-1'Hexagon; B- La tour Eiffel; C- La ville lumière
Exercise 3: A- faux ; B- vrai ; C- faux ; D- faux ; E- vrai

Leçon 9

Exercise 1: A-LUNDI; B- DIMANCHE; C- JUILLET ; D- MAI E-DÉCEMBRE ; F- AVRIL
Exercise 2: A- Sept; B- Douze

Leçon 12

Exercise 1: 1 A- L'orange; B- Le blanc; C- Le vert II A-le bleu; B- le blanc; C- le rouge

Leçon 13

Exercise 1: A- La tête ; B- L'œil; C- L'oreille; D- La main; E- Le pied

Leçon 14

Exercise 1: A-3; B-4; C-5; D-6; E-1; F-2

Leçon 15

Exercise 1: Paste the photos or write sport's activity along with name of student.

Leçon 16

Exercise 1: A- La chemise; B- Le chaussure; C- Le pantalon Exercise 2: A- La robe; B- Le sandale

Leçon 17

Exercise 1: A- La voiture; B- Le train; C- Le bus; D- Le vélo

Rappelons

Exercise 1: A- Le truck; B- Le jour de la mère ; C- Le calandrier ;D-Le hockey; E- Les grands-parents; F- Le ludo; G- Les cheveux; H-La; I- La jupe; J- Le péon
Exercise 2: A- mardi ; B- avril; C- février
Exercise 3: A- faux ; B- vrai; C- faux ; D- vrai; E-vrai

9 789369 917952

Printed at Repro India Ltd.